UNDERSTANDING WHEN
IT'S TIME TO LET GO
HOW I SAID GOODBYE TO MY PARENTS

ASHA SHAMKARRAN

authorHOUSE®

AuthorHouse™
1663 Liberty Drive
Bloomington, IN 47403
www.authorhouse.com
Phone: 1-800-839-8640

Published by AuthorHouse   05/10/2012

ISBN: 978-1-4772-0550-1 (sc)
ISBN: 978-1-4772-0549-5 (hc)
ISBN: 978-1-4772-0548-8 (e)

Library of Congress Control Number: 2012908679

I am glad that I was given the opportunity to be your child. Thank you, Mom and Dad for giving me life, for your love and guidance to help me be the woman I am today. For believing and trusting me to do what's right.

I love you both and miss you both very much and know that I will be OK for you are both showering me with your blessings.

Parenting can be the most stressful,

and most rewarding job of our life.

We do so many things

differently from our parents

and believe it

so too,

our kids will find ways to parent their children

differently from us.

MR. & MRS. GURDIAL RAMSARRAN
(EDDIE & ROSE)
MY PARENTS

YOU WERE LOVED
YOU ARE LOVE
AND
YOU WILL ALWAYS BE LOVE
BY YOUR CHILDREN,
GRANDCHILDREN
GREAT GRANDCHILDREN
SONS-IN-LAWS
AND
DAUGHTERS'-IN-LAWS

CONTENTS

Introduction...xix

We Were Lying..1

As Parents...9

Mom..17

Dad..25

Parent and Child Relationship....................................31

Community Person 37

Coping Without Parents 41

Accepting and saying good-by.....................................45

DEATH, GRIEF AND GOODBYES

Death of someone is never easy. It's very difficult when it's a love one and even worst when it's a parent.

We experience so much more grief and pain that we sometimes get mad at the entire world. We question ourselves, we sometimes even question the Lord, but we have to remember that death is the cycle of life. Someone is born and someone dies.

It's very difficult to predict how we will react when a parent dies for as a child we grew up believing that our parents are supposed to be around forever and ever.

Please allow me to share my experience of losing both my parents in an 18 months period. How I handle it and how I am able to deal with it on a daily basis as life goes on.

ACKNOWLEDGMENTS

To my husband and kids for
letting me be and giving me the space
to understand and deal with my feelings.
To my sisters and brothers
for their ongoing support of listening to me,
for always believing in me,
and not judging me.
Special thanks to the family and friends
for their love and support.

Om bhur bhuvah svah
tat-savitur varenyam
bhargo devasya dhimahi
dhiyo yo nah pracodayat

Twameva Mata, Chapita Twameva.
Twameva Bandhu, Cha Sakha Twameva.
Twameva Vidya, Dravinum Twameva.
Twameva Sarvam Mama Deva Deva.

O God,
You are my mother, my father, my brother, and my friend.
You are my knowledge and my only wealth.
You are everything to me and the God of all Gods.

INTRODUCTION

Years and years ago, as I was growing up, there were always two adults present around me. One, I called Daddy and one, I called Mommy, they were my parents.

I always taught that my parents were supposed to always be there for me forever and ever, whether I was grown up or not. They should help solve all the problems I would have to face in life, and they would be there in the good and bad times. They would never leave me. They would provide for me, everything that I needed or would need, as I was growing up.

As I got older and started school, I realized how much it took for my parents to always be around to assist and support us, which they did without any complain. Dad and Mom were there when I woke up in the morning, they were there when I went to school, they encouraged me to be careful and do my best. They were there when I came home from school, with snacks ready and they were there in the evening, sitting around until I finished my homework, just in case I needed their help.

As a young child, I was not a happy camper sitting night after night doing homework. I thought that homework was never fun and very boring. Then as I got older, I understood that when I did my homework, it was for my benefit. I will be the one who would benefit from it and be able to use my knowledge to make a better life for my family and myself. As I was got older I understood that my parents would not be there to forever hold my hand. I learnt that death will come to one and all and that I must learn as much as I can from my parents before it's too late. So, I quickly learned to use my parents as my role models. I wanted to mold my life into someone they would be proud of, and also someone that I will be proud of one day.

The last few decades have altered the images of my Dad and Mom. Their roles had changed, from being that of caregivers, to that of parents who needed our love, our caring, patience and support. They did their job of taking care for all their children, who are now all grown up and have families of their own.

They gave up everything, including their homeland to be closer to their children. As years went by, health and mostly age were catching up on them. So, as life continued, Mom and Dad became, having to be under our care instead of caregivers. Aging is a fact of life and it is also very difficult to handle without the love and support of one's family. Now as they get older we sometimes ask the question that we were always afraid to ask. Are they going to die anytime soon?

When a friend or someone we know lost a parent, we quickly expressed our sympathy. We said: 'I am so sorry for your loss and I can feel your pain. The pain will get better and you will always have those wonderful memories with you.'

WE WERE LYING

No one can feel or understand that pain unless you were or you are in that situation. There were friends and relatives that passed away in my family, I accepted them passing with less pain than what I felt when my parents passed away.

You see when I lost my mother I thought that my world was coming to an end. I cried every day and night for the good and sometimes for the bad memories. I could not pass by an ambulance. I would just cry. I was running from my car to her house, when the ambulance was taking her away, not knowing that she will be gone forever. I then and now understood what it was like to lose a parent, but I still had my Daddy.

Then, 18 months later my Daddy passed away. The hurting was more intense than before. Here I am, now without any parent, an orphan.

NO DAD, NO MOM JUST MY MEMORIES

So, we can share the sorrow, but until we are in that situation, we will never be able to understand one's true feelings of losing a parent.

When I was growing up, they were just my Dad and Mom. They were always there. Together, they worked in the fields and also had time left over for their children. They helped out in the community, helped a neighbor if need be, and other family members. They were always there for us when we got hurt, or when we did something good. They were also there when we did something wrong to discipline us for our own benefit. They were sincere in their protectiveness, their support and their responsibilities. They cared deeply for their children and worked very hard to be able to provide for us.

There is a saying that a father's job is to bring home the bacon. Well, both my parents took on that role. Together, they shared all responsibilities as far as their families and friends were concerned.

I think that I grew up not knowing if I respected or if I was afraid of my parents. Just a look from my Dad and I knew exactly what to do or how to behave. They taught us the good values and morals of life and how to use them to make a difference in our lives and others around us. They always put their children before everything else, never thinking about their wealth, happiness, health or prestige. They were two people living a life as perfect as one could. We, the children, were very fortunate to have been born to two such wonderful people, living their lives as an example to give us a chance to continue their legacy, a life of true devotion, honesty and respect for all.

They were loving parents, always ready to get involved in things that would make a difference for the well-being of their families. They would play games, cricket go to the park and such, but the most important of all was their willingness to help us grow intellectually and spiritually. They were always happy to sit and look at their children, grandchildren, and great grandchildren grow and prosper in their adventures in life. My parents were always ready to give advice, show their affection, concerns, and love for all, but never judging anyone. They were neither perfect nor faultless. They were simple and lived a simple life, but their hearts were rich.

I love my parents because they were always there for me. They were fun to be around and never intentionally caused their families any unhappiness. They shared my happiness and my sorrows without any judging or criticism but always had their love flowing.

My parents were both from very poor families. Daddy was the third child from a family of thirteen brothers and sisters and Mom was the second child of thirteen brothers and sisters. They had to work very hard to support their children and also assisted both sides of their families. I learned from my elder brother and sister about how tough life was for them when they had just gotten married, but they never gave up. Everyone on both sides of the families looked up to them, with love and respect. If ever anyone needed advice they always turn to Dad and Mom. They were always there in sickness, in happy times and in sad times to give whatever comfort and support that they could give.

They played a very big part in the various communities that they lived in. They were very spiritual, and encouraged growth of spiritually at home and in the communities. They lived their lives according to our spiritual book, 'The Bhagwata Gita'. They were true devotees of Lord Krishna.

My parents lived their lives to the fullest. They were very loving, committed and caring individuals. They were simple and lived as such. My parents loved each other very much. When my mother was alive she always told us that if my father died first she would go in that coffin with him. If they were unhappy about something, they never let us know or show it.

I understand that a day will come when we will have to leave this world. We all came into this world and we will also have to leave one day. Their deaths have left me feeling very empty at times, very lonely and very sad, but I know that they are my angels looking down on me. I miss their loving voices, their warn hugs and just about everything about them.

There are so many things that I want to share with them and believe me I do continue to talk to both of them very often, for I know that they are listening to me from somewhere above.

A PARENTS LOVE

I gave you life, but cannot live it for you.

I can teach you things, but I cannot make you learn.

I can give you directions, but I cannot be there to lead you.

I can allow you freedom, but I cannot account for it.

I can take you to church, but I cannot make you believe.

I can teach you right from wrong, but I cannot always decide for you.

I can buy you beautiful clothes, but I cannot make you beautiful inside.

I can offer you advice, but I cannot accept it for you.

I can give you love, but I cannot force it upon you.

I can teach you to share, but I cannot make you unselfish.

I can teach you respect, but I cannot force you to show honor.

I can advise you about friends, but cannot choose them for you.

I can advise you about sex, but I cannot keep you pure.

I can tell you the facts of life, but I can't build your reputation.

I can tell you about drinking, but I can't say "no" for you.

I can warn you about drugs, but I can't prevent you from using them.

I can tell you about lofty goals, but I can't achieve them for you.

I can teach you about kindness, but I can't force you to be gracious.

I can warn you about sins, but I cannot make you moral.

I can love you as a child, but I cannot place you in God's family.

I can pray for you, but I cannot make you walk with God.

I can teach you about the Lord but I cannot make Him your Lord.

I can tell you how to live, but I cannot give you eternal life.

I can love you with unconditional love all of my

life . . . and I will!!!

~Author Unknown

AS PARENTS

Being a good parent needs lots of love and courage, being open minded, flexibility and willingness to change and grow. Parents have to learn to incorporate the disappointments, loses, failures and pleasures into the healthy development of their children. A parent-child and a child-parent love is a bond no one in this world could take or replace. So, if ever there is a doubt, always remember that there is only one mother and one father in this world for us and they need our love as much as we need theirs. Without our love, compassion, understanding, listening, responsibility and concern for each other feelings, what would happen to our families when our parents are not around anymore? When we say that we love someone we not only have to say it but we also have to demonstrate actions that show that love.

sometimes wonder what it would have been like to not have had two such wonderful parents as my Dad and Mom. I read a book once where the person was saying that our parents are like our God; well my parents were truly my God. Dad and Mom was my first role model and now as a parent I hope that my children and grandchildren will use me as their role model.

Mom had a very special way with children. I remembered when my daughter was a baby and she used to take care of her. She used to spoil her in a good way. Mom and Dad always said that they spoiled their grandchildren because they did not have the opportunity to spoil their own children when they were small.

They were very involved in doing charitable work; like raising funds to help us keep our temple, helping anyone in the community whenever the need arose and taught us to do the same. Dad and Mom taught us that if we have respect for others then we will gain respect in return.

As far as I could remember they were always there for their children and families. I sometimes wonder if my parents thought that they would be together for so many years, have children, grand-children and great grand-children. Some of us do not even live to see so many years, but my Dad and Mom did it together. I know that Dad and Mom were very proud of us. If we the children and even outsiders look back, we will all be proud to have been part of their lives for they were the perfect role models for everyone. They were very simple and lived a simple life, not wanting too many material things to make them happy. They taught us to always be honest, respectable and loving. They taught us to always live a good life and to always follow our dreams.

I cannot remember a time when my parents were angry with each other. I am sure that they must have had their disagreements, but never in front of their children.

Growing up, I gathered how much my Dad loved cricket from various people but he always made sure that cricket did not affect his work or his responsibilities towards his families.

Moms took care of us kids and the home whenever she was not helping Dad. She never complained about working hard. They were a team from the beginning. Together they worked in the fields and shared the responsibilities of taking care of us as best as anyone in this world could have done.

I did not realized how important it was when my parents were setting boundaries for me but now I have enjoyed knowing that my they were concerned about my future. They taught me the difference and the consequences between right and wrong and about the values of religion. They taught me that my actions will have consequences; be it good or bad. They always stuck to their principles and gave us our space to make our own mistakes and to learn from them. They never tried to stifle our emotions but rather steer us towards something productive. I knew our boundaries and the stability and structure that I gained from them. I know that Dad and Mom loved me with all their heart. Their love made me feel valuable, worthy, and loved. Although I am responsible for my own life as an adult, Dad and Mom's advice meant the world to me and made me the woman I am today.

Mom was more-easy-going than Dad. He was very straight forward and just one look from him and believe me, we knew exactly how to act and behave. I remember one time when I was going to school and needed permission for a school trip and went to Mom, asking her if she would ask Dad for me. She told me to go ask Dad myself. I was so scared, I started crying and going over and over what I was going to say to Daddy. Eventually, I built up my courage and went. I had the hiccups, tears running down my face but no words were coming out of my mouth. Dad took one look at me and his face became serious. He asked me what I was crying for and when I did not answer him, he asked me if I needed a reason to cry. He then told me to go and when I was ready to talk to him then I could return. He did not look too happy because I was actually crying for nothing. Again, I rehearsed my speech, made up my mind and did it. I had to give Daddy all the details, where the trip was going, date, time, number of kids that were going and name and number of the teachers going with us.

After that, he told me it was ok. I was so happy that instead of walking, I was skipping to my room.

Mom would wake up very early in the morning to cook our breakfast and also lunch to take to school. During the time we were at school, she would help Dad in the rice field if there was work that needed to get done or they would work at the farm at home. There was also the poultry to be taken care of and whatever else was needed to get done. She would make sure that there were snacks ready for us when we returned from school and then had dinner ready. After we had our snacks, we had to do our chores and if there was time, we would play for a while. Sometimes my brother and I had to go help Dad at the rice field, which was sometime fun. After we had dinner, Mom would make sure the kitchen was clean and everything was put back in its place. Both Dad and Mom would sit around keeping us company as we were did our homework. Dad was around if we needed his intellectual assistance and Mom would do whatever odds and ends there was for her to do and make sure that there were some snacks for us, just in case one of us might need it.

As I was getting older I was given more responsibilities which helped instill in me desires to pursue my own interests and dreams.

Mom and Dad were our caregivers, always trying to do and gave us the best they could afford. They always gave us the things that we needed and not what we want.

can very clearly remember when I had my knee surgery. I could not get up and my family was either at work or at school. Dad would call me as soon as he thought that I was up to find out what time everyone would be leaving the house and he would make sure that he was over before they left. He made sure that I took my medication and had something to eat. He would sit so quietly watching the TV or reading the newspaper and not making a sound for he did not want to disturb me. After spending some time he would go back home knowing that Mom would, by then, be finished making something for him to bring for my lunch. Dad would come back bringing my nurse and my Mom, with him. She would help me take a bath and get me dressed, should anyone stop by as my family returned home.

Then when I had my shoulder operated on, they were both there to help again. This was a very special time and one that made me never ever second guess the love my parents had for me. They did everything as they did before, but because this time it was difficult for me to help myself being I am left handed and it was my left shoulder that was operated on. My Daddy fed me my soup. No questions were asked, he just did it and that moment will live in my heart until the day I die. They took care of me every single day until I was comfortable using my hand without hurting myself.

They were not only there for me during my illness but they were also there for my family when our son had a very serious accident. They gave my husband, daughter and myself the strength and love to carry on and not give up. They listened to us as we shared our pain, as we cried and answered questions as best as they could and never complained or judged us.

There was nothing much that anyone of us could have done as our parents aged but be loving, sensitive, have open communication and take care of them. Now, when I look at some movies that my parents liked or listen to the very old music that they used to listen to, it just brings back so many wonderful memories we shared together.

Most of the decisions I had to make so far in my life were based on teachings from my parents and the relationships I had with them. I always wanted my parents to be proud of me and as such, lived a good life. Because of the love and respect that my parents shared, I am now able to apply that in my life. My Dad and Mom had a very positive influence with me and I hope to pass that on to my children and grandchildren. Having them standing up to what they believed in made me who I am today.

As we learned about the hardships our parents had to face in their life, we the children, have to learn from it and appreciate our parents more and more. Just as we will do anything for our children, believe it or not, they were doing the same for us.

MY MEMORIES OF MOM

One of my happiest moments with Mom was her being there with me the day my daughter was born.

One of my saddest memories of Mom was seeing Mom getting weaker and weaker, the last few years of her life.

My last memory of Mom was how much fun I had playing with her the Wednesday before she died.

The thing I miss most about Mom is her funny side, her laughter, and most of all her love.

Things that Mom gave me that are important are the good values of life and how to use it to make a difference in the life of others.

I will always remember how hard Mom worked, her funny side, and her love for all of her children, grandchildren and great grandchildren and her family.

MOM

Being the second child of twelve brothers and sisters, Mom was unable to attend school much and at very early age had to drop out and work in the fields to help her parents support her family. She was married at a very early age into another large family where she also had to work very hard to help Daddy's family and together they had to continue helping her family.

Mom was a very loving, kind, generous, protective, neat, strong, religious, and over all, a very good person. I loved her protectiveness for her children. There were always teachings from her, "dress properly when you go out, or be careful of the company you keep." As I grew older, I saw how important her concerns were for my benefit and the benefit of my brothers and sisters.

Mom remained the loving, kind and good person all her life, no matter what hardship she had to face in life. She was always determined to conquer all obstacles and move forward and never complained about them. She was a very devoted wife and mother and always put the needs of her children in front of everything including her husband and herself.

After more than a decade of being separated we were again united in a foreign country and I was given a second chance to spend some time with them. As life continued with our share of problems, happiness, sorrows and everything else including age, Mom was diagnosed with Alzheimer's disease.

She needed someone around 24/7, and that was my Daddy. Her body had gotten very weak; so much so that moving around or doing little things for her-self, was very difficult. She was a baby all over again, needing the care instead of giving it. Mom sometimes talked to me about being confused and not knowing what she was doing. There were times when she was very frustrated for not being able to do anything for anyone or herself. I remember times when I would bring her over to my home and how difficult it was to get in the car. She would get so tired just walking from the garage into the house. All the simple things that she usually had done had become so difficult for her.

Although she was weak, her sweet lovingness was always there. I looked at her not being able to assist herself as a chance for me to take care of her and enjoyed her like a baby, as she did me. So, I continued enjoying my Mom for a few years until one day I had a phone call that changed my life.

I remembered the day my brother-in-law, who never call me, called at my job to tell me that Mom was sick and I needed to get home immediately. It was the worst moment of my life. I left work and the ten minute drive felt like one hour. As I was driving, I started reflecting on the memories of time I spent with my Mom. I remembered her loving nature, her playfulness with us, the grandchildren and the great grandchildren and her willingness to help others and lots more. I was crying, I was screaming and talking to myself all at once. By that time, after speeding through a school zone and stop lights, I reached her home.

The sight that greeted me tore my heart apart. There was the ambulance, fire truck and a few police cars. I started running, the ambulance started moving, and I screamed for it to stop "please do not take my Mother away, let me see her." It did not. Not knowing the situation, I then had to go inside the house and face my family and most fo all my Dad. As I was walking through the entrance, one of the police officers that I knew just shook his head and I immediately knew that I was too late. As I entered the house my little sister just grabbed me and shook her head. At that moment I would have given anything and everything that I had for anyone to tell me that Mom was ok, that she would be coming back home. How could she have left without saying good-by to me?

I talked to her just a few hours earlier and she was fine and happy for we were all going over that evening to celebrate Daddy's birthday. I understand that we come into this world and we also have to leave at some time, but I never thought that anytime was the right time for my parents to leave me. I did not want her to suffer and as such had to accept my loss and be strong, for I know that I will have to face another such day when I have to say goodbye to my Daddy.

Two days before Mom died, I decided to take time off from work and spend it with her, my two sisters, my brother, and Daddy. I gave her a bath, dressed her, and together we sat making jokes, eating and as the saying goes, "having a ball." We talked about the past, the present and the future. She asked about my grandchildren and demanded to see them, so I went and brought them over. She played with them. She had so much energy and did not want to take a nap as she usually does. We eventually put her in bed but she refused to close her eyes. Her love for us was just shining, no worries, even for herself. She was just enjoying the time with us. She told us that if she goes to sleep she will be missing out on what we will be saying to Daddy. We spent a few more hours and I went home so that she could take a nap. That was the last time I saw my Mom alive.

I know that my Mom had to die sometime, but not this suddenly. Intellectually, I was somewhat prepared, but emotionally, I was ready to explode. There were so many different emotions, I was sad, I was nervous, I was angry, I was afraid, I was worried, I was confused, I was numb and I was in denial. I wanted to scream but was ashamed that others might think that I am weak. I tried to hide my feelings and be brave. I did not want anyone, especially my brothers and sisters, to know that I was falling apart. A few days later all the arrangements were made and Mom was cremated.

The service was held, the viewing was done, and then the coffin was transported to the cremation site. I did not want to be there and I also did not want her to be there. Then, the moment came for my brother to press the button. It felt like he was pushing a button in my heart. I tried to be brave, but suddenly, I felt my body very light and the next thing I remembered was being in the car, on our way back home, without my Mom.

Back at the house the family was all gathered together, trying to pull our strength from each other. We stayed a few more days with our Dad and eventually the day came when my sisters and myself had to go back to our homes. It was so difficult, for we had to leave our Daddy all alone to start a new chapter in his life without Mom, his life-long partner.

As time went by, I was still unable to talk to anyone or share my feelings with anyone. Eventually, I closed everyone out even my husband and children. I was embarrassed to ask for help, I wanted them to comfort me without any questions. After a few months I eventually shared my feelings with an outsider who advised me to speak to my family and let them know how I was feeling and not to just assume how they would react towards me. She said that if and when I shared my pain, only then I would be able to let my Mom go and find peace within myself.

Then, after Mom's one year memorial, my brothers, sisters, and Dad all got together and shared how we were coping with Mom not being around. I told them how I felt and got so much loving support from everyone, including my Dad. We were all grieving and handling it in our own way, but just being able to share and understand that we could always depend on each other's love and understanding was a very big comfort. I was able to feel more at peace with myself and let my Mom go and be in peace.

My Mom is dead and gone but her loving memories will live with me forever and ever. I hope that one day I will be able to get passed the pain I feel for losing the most wonderful Mother in this world. I know that the pain will never go away but hopefully, with time, it will be replaced by only happy memories.

I LOVE YOU MOM

MY MEMORIES OF DADDY

One of my happiest moments with Dad was the Friday evenings, that he usually spent with me.

One of my saddest memories of Dad was the day we lost my Mom.

My last memory of Dad was the Monday morning before he passed away. We were talking about my daughter getting ready to leave home for the first time and he shared some of his words of wisdom that comforted me.

The thing I miss most about Dad is the way he would listen and advices me, without ever judging me.

Things that Dad gave me that are important, are the good values of life and how to use them to make a difference in my life, that of others, and the importance of our spiritual lives.

I will always remember how hard Dad worked, his wisdom, his willingness to always help others and the love for all of h is children, grandchildren, and great grandchildren.

DAD

Daddy was the third child of twelve brothers and sisters. He came from very poor parents who did farming for a living. As such, Dad also became a very proud and happy farmer. He had to work very hard to assist his parents, brothers and sisters. After he got married, he also helped in planting and harvesting the crops for Mom's family.

Dad was very stern, honest, loving, protective, and adventurous. He loved reading and as such, he was very knowledgeable and self taught himself. When we were going to school, there was never a question we asked him that he was unable to assist us with. He made sure that all of his children had a very good education. Dad once said that "it is not how much we learn but what we learn." Dad used his knowledge to help us grow and enrich our lives.

Daddy loved sports especially cricket. He always shared how he and my uncles used to play when they were younger. He would always give my nephews advice and hints on how to be a good cricketer. He would stay up all night looking at a game on TV, and whenever he meets anyone that loves cricket that's would be the first topic of conversation.

He loved to travel and see different places. He embraced life's challenges to the fullest. Dad taught me how to love life and live it to the fullest. He helped me understand that life is a challenge and full of adventures. He taught me to never give up, that everything that happens; happens for a reason, a reason that we must learn to grow from.

Dad was many things in my eyes. He was my best friend, my Dad, a good listener, counselor, whatever the circumstance, that's the hat he would put on. He was always ready to give assistance to anyone. He was independent, and was able to take care of himself without assistance from anyone.

During Mom's last few years, he was so loving and caring to her everyday needs, never thinking of himself and always putting her happiness first until the day she died. That was the day Daddy completely gave up on life. Daddy told me that he was finished with his job that he was sent on earth to do and was now ready to go and serve the Lord.

After Mom died, my relationship with my Daddy changed. I realized that Dad was the only parent left and needed me more, for he had to adjust his life to living without this loving person whom he had been sharing his life with. Dad became more and more depressed, not wanting to leave the house and go anywhere. We never gave up. We continued trying to get him involved in things and after a few months we taught that he was adjusting to this new chapter without Mom.

Then eighteen months later, in the middle of the night my phone rang, and we all know that a phone call in the middle of the night is never good. I felt my body go cold, here it goes. I was told to meet my brother at the hospital for Dad was having chest pains and he was being taken by an ambulance. For a few moments I was unable to move, I just screamed. 'No Daddy, not you Daddy.' I, then, got dressed as quickly as possible and met the rest of my family at the hospital. Daddy was by then taken into the emergency room and only one person was allowed to be with him, so we took turns.

Then, it was my turn. There, lying on the bed was my Daddy, a man who never complained about pain, was in so much pain that he could not lie still on the bed. I knew that something was desperately wrong with my Dad. I wanted to scream. He was looking at me with this empty look and told me that he was having so severe pains and that it was moving around in his chest. I begged him to hold on. that my brother was getting the doctor. I did not like the thoughts that were going through my mind and the condition my Daddy was in, so I came out and sent my little sister to see Dad. After a few minutes she came out and just by looking at her we knew that something was seriously wrong with our Daddy. There were tears in her eyes and her hands were shaking. She told us that the doctor needed to speak to us in the family conference room.

So, together we were escorted to the room. We went in and the doctor explained that there was nothing more they could do for Daddy and we had to just wait and see. They told us that they were going to give Daddy some medicine to help him with the pain so that he would be able to relax a little better. We were then allowed to go into his room and spent the last few hours with him.

He was hooked up to machines with his eyes closed and I wanted to scream for him to get up and let's go home. The intellectual part of me knew that there was nothing I could do but the emotional part was already screaming for I was about to lose another love one. Dad was not sick, so there was no sign that death was so nearby for him, for he was doing fine a few hours earlier.

I did not stand and watch my Mom pass away, so you can imagine what it was like for me to stand and watch my Daddy slowly and slowly leave this world. We all gathered around his bed, touching various parts of him in loving hope that our love connected and we started chanting prayers on Daddy's behalf. I wanted to scream but I did not want him to know that I was sad. I wanted him to open his eyes and look at us, to say something, anything, any movement, but he just laid there on the bed, so peaceful as if he was sleeping. I talked to the Lord, 'please god tell me this is not happening, please do not let this happen. Please do not let my Daddy suffer for He is a very true devotee to You, O Lord. Please let him not linger on the machine for too long if you are ready to take Him to Your home. Why so quickly after our mother, O Lord.?

We all whispered our little goodbyes for we knew that Daddy was slowly and slowly leaving us. We then started chanting the name of the Lord until it was finally the time for him to leave us. At that moment, nothing came out of me, not a sound, not even a tear. The room was quiet except for the sound of the machines. No one moved or said anything. I felt my entire world collapse, taking with it a bigger piece of me, this time around. Eventually, the machine slowly stopped and Daddy was gone forever and ever.

Leaving Daddy in that room, knowing that he was no longer alive was the hardest thing for me to do. He looked so peaceful, no longer in pain, as if he was just sleeping. I knew that this was the last time I would ever be able to look at my Daddy again.

As we left his room, consoling each other, my thoughts were on my two brothers that were not present, for both of them were now missing out in saying goodbye in person, to both their parents. My two brothers were not as fortunate as we were to be by our parents' side at the time of their death.

That moment of letting go was the hardest thing I had to face, for when Mom died, I was not there. I did not stand and watch as her soul left her body. All the grief that I was feeling for my Mom automatically transferred to my father. My grief was combined in one big parcel. I know that we all came into this world and that we all have to leave someday. So, I had to let my Daddy go.

Again, all the families came to support us and arrangements were made for Daddy to be cremated a few days later. The service was held, the viewing was done and the day of the cremation came. I begged God to give me the strength to be strong for that was the last promise that I made my Dad. Then, the moment came for my brother to press that button again. I closed my eyes for I did not want to see the coffin rolled away for I knew that was the end of me having any parent ever again.

Daddy was a very kind, sensitive, loving, compassionate and honest person. He taught us the values of life and encouraged us to use them to make a difference in our lives.

I LOVE YOU DADDY

PARENT AND CHILD RELATIONSHIP

Communication between parents and children is a job that is never easy. When we were younger we never wanted to understand that whatever our parents were saying and doing was for our own good but as we got older and had a family of our own—IT HIT US. 'That's what Mom and Dad used to say or do.'

There were times when we did not understand the reason why they wanted things done their way, but as we got older the reason becomes clearer. Our open communication prevented us from having any major differences with our parents. We knew that winning an argument was never important as our relationship with our parents. There were times when Dad would argue a point with one of us kids but there was always a common ground reached at the end. We were always allowed to express ourselves and being respected for it. Because of our open communication, we were able to enjoy the closeness with our parents and able to understand them and their needs. Whenever we were able to all be together, we always put aside a few hours to sit with our parents and share what was happening in our lives, be it good or bad. We asked for their advice and opinion on things that we could not handle on our own.

Mom and Dad were very good listeners and always gave their advice and let us make our decisions. Because of this open relationship, we were able to benefit from Dad's experiences and his wisdom.

It's sometimes too difficult to accept that our parents were getting older and needed their children help. We always wanted to believe that they would remain strong, active and always be there to take care of us. We wanted them to be there in good times to acknowledge us and also in bad times to help solve our problems.

It was so important that as our parents got older, that we their children, showed them our love and kept our communication with them open and as simple as possible. As grown children we were responsible to take care of our parents, and I am very proud to say that my parents had given me that opportunity.

When we were young kids growing up, Dad and Mom gave us food and shelter, took care of our health and education. As young adults they gave us love, support, and advice whenever we allowed them to. When we became adults and ran into any difficulty, we again turned to them for their assistance, love and guidance. It was our responsibility to take care of our parents as they got older, regardless of the situation. Whatever way Dad and Mom brought us up, the past never influenced our responsibilities.

My Dad and Mom always put our needs first, as we were growing up, and as an adult, whenever I asked my parents for advice or assistance; they never had to think twice before offering their help to me. Dad and Mom always communicated what they expected from us, with love and affection, and that allowed us to strive to meet those expectations.

As my parents were getting up there in age there was never a thought in neither my head nor my brothers' and sisters' minds that we should think of putting them in a nursing home. We were all willing to make adjustments to our daily life to assist when Mom needed the assistance. Daddy was with her 24/7. There are pros and cons to having a loved one put in a nursing home but we knew that mommy would be better with us at home.

There was someone that I knew who took her father to a nursing home just because she thought that he needed help and she was working and did not want strangers in her house. She did not think that her father may not get the proper care, may become depressed, unhappy, and most of all get lonely and missing his family. We sometimes forget that our parents put their lives on hold just to take care of us, make sure that if something was bothering us, to help in whatever way they could. They sometimes helped us take care of our children and most of all they had never, never let us fall, and if we did they were there to pick us up. So, we need to do our duty and be responsible adults, as our parents taught us to be. We must accept the fact that as both a parent and a child gets older, we the child must be more protective, loving, sensitive and caring towards them.

By taking care of our parents we were setting a very good example to our children, and it may be to our benefit when we get to our parents' age. We will not have to wonder about open communication as parent and child, or if we will have to live in a nursing home or will we be cared for, will there be someone around if we get sick, and will we be able to share in our children and grandchildren success. If we do not act as role models for our children, we may someday find ourselves very lonely and sad.

Lots of times our aged parents may not want to ask for help, for they sometimes feel that if they do they will lose their children respect. We had to listen closely to what they were saying.

We had to be part of their lives, for example; taking them to the doctor, let them have visitors. Our attitudes towards our parents surely make a big difference on how well they accepted getting old.

Only through open communication were we able to assist our parents in the quality of life as they were getting older. They were always supportive, helpful to everyone regardless of the circumstances. They were very devoted to the community and always did charity work to help, and they did so just because it was the correct thing to do.

I had a wonderful and open relationship with both my parents especially my Dad. Because of my Moms illness the last few years it was very difficult to communicate everything with her. I was able to share everything with my Dad.

Now, I sometimes look back at the relationship I had with my parents as I was growing up and compared it to the relationship we had for the last two decades with me being an adult. I wondered what happened to that very straight forward couple I grew up with for in their old age they have mellowed out so much. They were more calm, quiet, gentle and loving.

Growing up I never imagined Dad carrying a grandchild on his shoulders to the park, but I saw it when my daughter was a baby. She actually lived with Mom and Dad and during that time they were so proud and carried her everywhere. They had so much love and patience with her.

Four days before my Dad passed away he was saying farewell to this very granddaughter and as I stood by with tears in my eyes, my Dad turned to me and said, 'Do not cry for your child, wish her well, pray for her and be proud of her. She is much older that you were when you left home. How do you think I was feeling at that moment to send you so far away?'

I was shacked beyond words for I never taught that my leaving home affected my Dad that much. Now that I am a parent I am able to understand my parent feelings

COMMUNITY PERSON

Not everyone can be a leader. To be a good leader one has to have good qualities and work towards the benefit of the community as a whole and not for his or her own personal gain and reward. They have to be considerate and polite to their neighbors. They have to value others and stand up for what is right. They have to be able to take on responsibilities that will improve the community. My Daddy and Mom were those persons.

Dad was chosen as a leader of the community, that we lived in, by the people. Together, with Mom by his side, Dad was chosen for his values and passions, as he had a strong sense of integrity, knowing and doing only what was right. Dad was always willing to listen to ideas and concerns from any and all in the community. He always had a big picture of the things they could do in the community and there was the willingness and responsibility to make it happen. Dad and Mom had a lot of courage and confidence in whatever project they took on, that it would be done on time and to the best of their ability. Dad's intelligence, wisdom and flexibility helped him to interact and work with the people of the community. Whatever project Dad took on in the community, my Mom was there by his side all the way. She had the strength and will power to follow him. They were both very spiritual and, as such, encouraged and promoted spirituality to everyone who was willing to accept it.

My parents were both very kind and always ready to give a helping hand when someone needed it. I remember when someone in the neighborhood got sick, they always came to our house to see if my Mom had some medicine they could use. Mom, even sometimes took a neighbor to the doctor if they needed medical attention. One evening when I was visiting my parents, we heard kids shouting, 'thief, thief, Uncle Eddy, help us." My dad, without giving a second thought started running to that home. He did not stop to think that it was dark, or to ask someone to go with him, or to check if any other neighbor was coming out of their home. He did not give it a thought that he could have gotten killed. He just ran. That was the kind of person that he was.

If they told you that they were going to help you do something, you can bet your last dollar that they would fulfill their promise at whatever cost. If someone in the community had a function and needed help, Dad and Mom were always there to give a helping hand. When there was planting and harvesting of the rice crop, Dad was always there helping whomever needed his help and they, in return, would help him. Dad also helped the youths in the community to form a youth organization and become involved in doing things to benefit themselves as well as the community.

They both always found the time to get the community together for fun events. Dad usually organized fund raisers for the temple in our community. Daddy, together with a few of the neighborhood men, would get together and decide on a date, place and time they thought would be all right for everyone. They would decide on the games, music, and social events to take place, and ordered whatever they needed. Mom, together with other ladies, would get together and plan the menu, and decided on what was needed to buy. Then, on the day of the event, Dad and the men would go set up, while the ladies would come over to our home and help Mom with the cooking. Then they would all gather at the park and assisted wherever they were needed. They never got paid for their services; all that was done was given from their hearts.

Dad and Mom were respected in the community by all age groups. I remembered when I was going to school and if someone wanted to speak to me, they would not, if they knew my parents, and the ones that did not know my parents just had to hear their names and they would just disappear.

Daddy had the ability to guide the youths in our community to take on positive roles that would enrich their lives as well as those in the community. He gave the youths a chance to make decisions and be responsible for the consequences of their decisions. Daddy always believed that youths needed proper guidance to help them to become adult leaders and also make a difference in their lives as they got older.

Many a time I wondered how they were able to do so many things for the community and also take care of everything else at home.

COPING WITHOUT PARENTS

It's so easy to deny that our parents were getting older, weaker and needed their children' support more. That's every child's duty, which many any of us sometimes ignore. For some of us, losing a parent leaves us empty, with lots 'what ifs'. There is sadness, fear, feeling cheated, shocked, depression, denial, pain, anger and sometimes even guilt.

When a parent dies our life is changed forever, for without them our lives would not be possible. They are responsible for who we are. Our sense of security is torn and our family will never be the same again. My life will not be the same but hopefully I can improve my outlook on life with the help, guidance and teachings that I received from my parents.

My parent's death left me very emotionally drained. I understand that we come into this world and we also have to leave it at some point. I was, and I am ok with that, but sometimes my heart takes over and the pain of losing Mom and Dad just flows through me, causing so much sadness. There were days when I could not remember anything I did for their thoughts clouded my mine. I accept the loss of my parents but will never forget them. Their birthdays, wedding anniversary, death anniversary and family get-togethers will be so difficult but I hope that with my family support that this too will get easier with time. I missed Mom and Dad's love, support, and guidance but will always have fond memories of them to help me along the way.

As I am accepting the loss of both my parents it does not mean that I love them any less. It's just that I know that this is life and it has to go on, and their memories will always be there in my heart. Now, when I am feeling sad and missing them, I recollect the happy times that we shared together. Listening to their favorite songs, seeing an old movie that they loved, sharing their teachings, are some of the memories that will live with me forever. I learned that sharing my feelings did not mean that I was a weak person. It just helps to ease the pain. I knew that I could not do it alone anymore, so the sharing, having faith and communication is really helping me. It is painful because of the excellent relationship my parents and I had.

I am very grateful to all my family for sharing their stories and memories of my parents with everyone. It's time like this that we really understand how much we need our families, friends and love ones. There are so many things that we take for granted when our loved ones are alive, and suddenly that love one is gone and those things becomes our cherished memories. The grieving comes unexpected, and at odd times, but when they did, I called one of my sisters and shared my feelings and even cried if I had to with her.

I am grateful for the life they gave me and the love they showed in bad and good times. They will always be with me as though they have never left me. I pray to them to please shine down on me and help me though the bad and hard times and help me to be a better person.

It's never easy to lose a parent. My relationship with Mom and Dad was very special, so losing them was and is very difficult for me. They were in my life forever, for as long as I can remember. So, now there is some sadness, but I found out that if

I smile when I remember them and have faith that they are both with the Lord, I find myself more at peace.

Dad and Mom were like a circle, holding the entire family together and I know that my brothers and sisters will follow in our parents' footsteps and keep united forever and ever. We are all children of the same parents and we mourn our loss differently, but if we keep sharing our feelings, the pain of our loss will be easier to carry.

Thank you, Lord, for the two most wonderful people you gave me as my parents and the cherished memories that we shared during our time together. I thank the Lord each and every day for giving me the opportunity to share so many years with my parents, for there are lots of others who are not so lucky.

ACCEPTING AND SAYING GOOD-BY

I know that death comes to everyone, we are born and we must die, but emotionally we sometimes do not want to accept it. I did not. We try to make deals with the Lord.

When I was growing up Mom and Dad were both always around. They helped see me through school, see me through the good and the bad times, through sickness and they had been there to give their advice whenever I needed it. Even though they were getting on in years, just their presence and support made a difference and gave me allot of peace of mind.

Now that both of them are dead and gone, their presence is no longer here and life has been a little empty. I still handle all problems by myself and solve them as best as I can, but the support, advice and loving attention from Mom and Dad is no longer there. I appreciate them now more than ever before.

After Mom died, I was very distracted from my life. I was falling apart and did not know how to handle her loss and most of all I kept everything to myself and was not sharing it with my family, brothers, and sisters and even with Daddy. Then, Daddy died and my world collapsed. For the first few months everything I was doing, was done just because I had to and not with any care as to how it was getting done. My friend, my teacher, my advisor, MY DADDY was no more. I can now accept my loss and continue to move on with my life, full of their memories. I AM NOW AN ORPHAN.

Some of us handle death better than others, and some feel that one should grieve only for a period of time and you get reluctant to open up and share your feelings. Even the strongest sometime become the weakest at time of grief.

I remember at both my parents' funerals how the family was sharing their memories of Mom and Dad with each other. I laughed, I cried, and I was even shocked to learn of the hardship my parents had to endure to be able to give us everything we needed and also assisted the family whenever possible. I remembered, at Mom's funeral, how one of my aunts was sharing how Mom had to leave school at a very early age to help work in the fields and support her brothers and sisters. She continued assisting even after she was married and had her own children to take care of. They shared her funny side and always made people laugh and be happy. Her helpful side was to always be willing to do whatever it took to assist anyone who asked for her help. Her major contribution to the community was as a good listener, giving good advice, willing to assist in way to improve the community. She was a spiritual person and contributed very much to help promote and assist Daddy in his adventure of making a difference in helping others. At Daddy's funeral, his sisters were sharing how he was very strict, his love for cricket, how he and his brother and friend would go to the movie and came home before my grandfather realize that they were gone. They shared with us about his love for his family and some of the things he did to keep their family together. They shared Daddy's devotion to the Lord and how he always worked with the community he lived in to grow spiritually and lovingly. Those are some of the memories that I will have to feed on to keep them alive and vibrant in my heart forever.

The families and friends were very supportive, helpful and sympathetic to us. My brothers, sisters and I were all like robots, getting all the arrangements made without feeling anything for we were all numb. At first I felt as if I was going crazy, for I was unable to share my feelings. After, the families went back to their homes, I had to do the same and move on, for I could not expect them to be there with us forever.

Death is a must, it is final, no one can revoke it and no one accepts it. It is difficult to deal with and every one of us handles it differently. Everyone that dies has a connection to us but when it's a parent, that pain, and loss is totally different. The bond of a parent and child is totally different, from that of a brother, sister, uncle, aunt, child, grandparents or even a close friend. If shared, the pain becomes less. I felt as if the time that I had with them was just a dream, that it was not real. When they were alive I felt very secure for they were always around to keep our family together.

Saying goodbye to my parents was very difficult and I must remember that my children will one day be in the same situation as I am.

We must use our relationship with our parents to mold the relationship we have with our children. We must remember that as we watched our parents aged, we are also aging and our children also age. So the cycle of life must continue. We were the caregivers to our parents and now that we are aging we are hoping that our children become our caregivers. Some of us may not be as lucky as others to have their children as caregivers. We hope that through the aging process we are able to be independent and will be able to take care of ourselves until our last day.

Death may bring a family together and can also destroy a familys' bond forever. Death of a parent causes all different kinds of feelings: fear, sadness, anger, denial, feeling cheated, depressed, shocked, numbness and helplessness. We have to gradually be able to deal with these feelings and continue moving on. Death is a must and parents must never want their children to grieve forever. They will want their children to bond with each other more than ever before. They will want their children to continue their legacy and make them proud. Death makes one think very carefully about life and make changes as to how they want to live out the rest of their lives. Death does not tell us what time is the right time, where or how it will happen. It can happen so suddenly and without any warning. We ask God that it's not fair for us to lose anyone we love so much, so why take away my parent? Why do you let us love one another so much and then in a second you take them away? At the time of our loss it seems all-right for all the different thoughts and questions to run through our mind but we have to use them to build up our strength. Death is inevitable and it will happen again, for we do not have any control over it.

Death is a time for bonding and sharing our feelings. It's a time to come together and grieve. It's a time to look up to someone else as a parental figure, not to replace your parent, but just to have a substitute to lean on.

When a parent dies all the remorse and questions starts to pop up. Life is like a road with rocks and pebbles on one side and on the other side there are rows and rows of all different colors of beautiful flowers. As we are walking along this road we will tend to ignore the side with the rocks and walk along the side with flowers. We may even pick a few of the flowers and enjoy its beauty and sweet smell. It's the same with life. As we travel this path, let's pick up, if not all, some of the good teachings that our parents left with us and follow them to make our life a better one.

We need to put aside all differences and be the loving children our parents will want us to be. They were our parents and whatever they did for us, they did as best as they knew how. There may be times that we did not like their rules but putting ourselves in their shoes, as parents, we will probably do exactly the same. We let a very small dispute keep us away from each other, but a single phone call in the middle of the night and there will be regrets forever. When a parent is dead we are willing to give up everything, do anything to bring them back, but it does not work that way.

All, most parents need from us as adult children, are our loving understanding and to see us live a life that they would be proud of. Being involved in their lives in their old age is a comfort and a blessing to them for it would be sufficient because of the way they brought us up. It's not necessary to wait for a funeral to let people know how much we love and appreciate them. Let's do things to show them our love and appreciation, let's communicate with them, past, present and future. That's the only way that we will be able to learn more about our parents, and in doing so, cherish the memories when it's time to say goodbye.

A funeral is a time for grief and a time to say a final goodbye. It's a time to be complete with losing a loved one and realizing that it's the last time we will be seeing that face and body. Seeing them again will be in memories we carry of them. It's a time for everyone to share their experiences with the person that passed away. It's a chance to learn a little more about his or her life. It's a time for families to show their love and hopefully let the past be the past and remember that tomorrow may be one of us lying in that coffin. We must remember that we come into this world and we must also leave one day, but our actions and the things we do will be the memories that we left behind. We as children had to live a life that reflected the teachings that we got from our parents and make their legacy live on.

My parents were remembered for their kindness to everyone they met, families, friends and also people that just heard about them. Everyone that came to their funeral had something good to share with us about them. I cannot think of anything bad when I think of them. All my memories are so wonderful. I was and I am very fortunate to have been born to two such wonderful parents. I think of it as a blessing to be able to grow up with them as my role models. I am the person I am today because of them and as such I am able to pass their teachings to my children and grandchildren.

The death of my parents left me feeling empty and lonely. The two people, who never judged me, offered me love, support and understanding, no matter what, are now gone. I know that the pain will gradually heal and that I will discover my inner strength to help me, but the memories and time shared will live on forever and ever in our hearts.

I have tried to hold on to my parents but I woke up one day and realized that I had to let them go, to let their soul rest in that beautiful garden of Bhagwan Krishna. There are good days and there are some bad days. There are days when I will just cry thinking about them, looking at a picture or a movie, or listening to a song that they liked. I sometimes called out to them. There are times when I just wanted to feel their arms around me, giving me the biggest hug possible, or to hear their voices. Then there are days when those things that usually make me sad, bring me so much peace, joy and happiness.

Now that I have gone through the grieving process of both my parents I am able to understand and share in the pain of others. There may still be times that I may not know the right thing to say but being able to understand may help them to heal. For me, the best healing medicine is being brave enough to share my feelings and thoughts with my family. I thought that if my family knew how I was feeling, they would think that I am crazy, but I was so wrong. With their love and support I am able to continue on a daily basis with memories of my parents and with less pain. Mom and Dad are now in a very happy place looking down on me. I know that with this thought inside my heart, I will live with their memories, carry out their legacy and happy for them.

After my Mother died I became closer to my Daddy for I realized that time for our separation is just around the corner. I dreaded the day but knew that Dad did not want to be around. He always said that he did his duty and wanted to go and be with Mom and the Lord. I know that I did my duty as a daughter and hope and pray that they will both be there, waiting for me when my time comes, with loving open arms.

Without any doubt or question in my mind, Dad and Mom were the best teachers we could have had. They listened to us, respected us, heard what we were saying and valued our opinions, never judging us and instilling dignity in us.

I missed my parents very, very much. There are still times that I get mad at the entire world for losing both of them. I look at myself in the mirror and I can see a younger version of my mother.

Thank you Dad and Mom for helping me to be the person I am today. Thank you for helping me to be a good role model for my children and grandchildren and others around me. You both have lived your lives by the book and I thank you for showing me that that's the only way to live my life.

You taught me to accept everyone for who they are and not judge them.

You taught me that whatever I do I must do as best as I can.

You taught me to never forget the Lord and to keep growing spiritually.

You taught me to live a good life, enjoy it, respect it, take the challenges (good, bad, pain, sufferings) that come with it, and dance to its music.

You were wonderful, affectionate loving, compassionate, sensitive, and most of all you were the greatest parents anyone could ask for. You have given your life to your children and now we promise you both that we will live up to your legacy and make you proud of us.

I missed Mom and Dad dearly and would give anything to hear their voices, hear them laugh, them giving me advice or a big hug or just having their presence near me. I hope and pray that their teachings help us all to live a life that they would be proud of if they were alive. The healing period has its highs and its lows but I am making it through each day knowing how much they loved me.

We all miss you every day and wonder why our lives had to be changed in this way. You were our rocks, our confidants, our supporters. In death we love you as much as in life.

Smile upon us and help keep us strong. Mom & Dad, all of us are doing well; you raised us to be strong. We will live keeping your legacy alive forever. We know that you are together in heaven.

Since Mom and Dad died, I found that devoting more of my time to the Lord is healing the grief and as such I now more devoted to grow spiritually. For this I am very grateful.

I learned that one of the ways to help me cope with my loss was by expressing it. So, writing this book has allowed me to have so much more peace and less pain when remembering Mom and Dad.

I LOVE YOU BOTH ALWAYS

SOMEONE TOLD ME THAT

YOU ARE BOTH SLEEPING IN THE

ROOM NEXT DOOR, SO

GOOD NIGHT MOM AND DAD.

I LOVE YOU

BOTH VERY, VERY MUCH

We are all scared of losing our parents at any time in our lives for as a child we think that parents are supposed to live on forever and ever. But as life goes on we learn that this is not true. They will have to die sometime and so too will us.

We will grief, we will cry, we will laugh but we have to remember that a parent will never want for their child to always grief for them. A parent will want their child to move on and live a life that they would have been proud of.

We are alive for a reason. It's not our time as yet. There are things that still need our attention and until we complete them, we have to remain here in this world.

Parents that are now gone, have done the job they were sent here to do. So, it's our turn to do the job we were sent here to do.

Let us always remember that they are only gone physically for their memories will live on with us for as long as we are here, and it's up to us to share those memories with our children so that the family legacy will continue on.

Be patient, be strong and have faith in the Lord to handle everything as it's written for us.